Introduction

Since 2001 I have been a member Birmingham's largest writers group, *Writers Without Borders*, and I've been the figurehead of the group since 2008. There are about 27 members and I've loved and appreciated every interesting and inspiring moment. Working and developing together as a group has enabled us to grow individually as writers and performers, but also as WWB collective, making us what we are today!

I would like to take this opportunity to thank each and every one for trusting me and allowing me to be part of your experience, not forgetting all those who have supported and guided WWB along our creative journey.

This anthology, a progressive repertoire of food-for-thought page-turning encounters of words, represents the quintessential journey of the writers. This collection of poems and prose conveys the energy and elements needed to grasp the reader's interest and perhaps manifest a smile. We hope you will be inspired and that it will help you to embrace, to learn, or to simply appreciate and respect the powers of the creative imagination…

So merely turn the page and read on aloud….

or just stream the words and rhythms quietly within!

Give thAnks

Sue Brown

Dear Colin

I am very privileged to be part of your group. Wish you all the best

Shri

ISBN 978-1-326-42973-7

© 2015 Writers Without Borders. All rights reserved.

Copyright to individual pieces of work are held by the authors as named for each.

Further copies available from Lulu.com - ID number 17351261

Contents

Contents 3
'Femi Abidogun 4
Jude Ashworth 8
Patricia Bamurangirwa 12
Rashida Begum 16
Sue Brown 20
Keisha Diamond 24
Predencia Dixon 28
Inge Durrani 32
Ita Gooden 36
Nabila Jameel 40
Tessa Kate Lowe 44
Ahmed Magare 48
Barbara Peterson 52
Shirin Ramzanali Fazel 56
David Rollason 60
Sindy Stanley 64
Sayyara Syed 68
Martin Underwood 72
Farideh Valigholizadeh 76
Fiona Wallace 80
Elaine Yap 84
Vivian Yates 88

'Femi Abidogun

I was born in Ibadan, Nigeria and have been a member of *Writers Without Borders* since February 2012.

To date I have two published collections of poetry (*That Long Walk* - 2015 and *Blonde Grass*- 2012 both published by Thynks Publications Ltd, Nottingham).

My writings have also appeared in a number of publications and I recently featured on BBC West Midlands where I had the opportunity to talk about my writings as well as to read from my latest book.

My writings are majorly influenced by my environment, background, experiences (both mine and others) and general happenings. For me, writing is all about expression and it is that unique opportunity to express without being inhibited that endears me to it; that opportunity to allow emotions, experiences, feelings and thoughts to be expressed aptly via the stringing together of carefully selected words.

Apart from writing I also enjoy reading, travelling, music and sports.

I am married with children.

Calling a Night a Day

"Look at a day when you are supremely satisfied at the end. It's not a day when you lounge around doing nothing; it's a day you've had everything to do and you've done it."
— Margaret Thatcher

The snug warmth of my duvet beckons
"Come on"
It says as it urges me on
To feel the softness of its contours
And test run its ability
To instantly
Drive me straight up and land
Me on the doorways of dreamland.
The solemness of this night
Plays its own part
And reminds me that the time is right
To quit.
The quiet and aura around
Utter loud,
Silent words that cry at my jaded face
"It's time to lay your head on a safe place".
But work, I must work
Not just to leave leavened bread on my plate
But to reach that point
Where I can confidently thump my chest
And proudly say
That so much I had to do
And now it's all a done deal.

Boomerang

Today, it seemed time was doing the sprints. Every minute seemed to fly away, at least, according to Dale's new *Roylex* wristwatch - a crudely crafted *wannabe* of the Swiss Rolex. Knowing the journey to the big city was going to last another two hours, he spoke to the bus driver on the need to begin the journey forthwith. He just could not afford to miss his all-important job interview.

Like many of his mates, Dale had endured the pains of unemployment. It seemed all the employers he sent his applications to had the same ready-made responses:"...we are sorry but your qualifications and experience do not match what the role requires...". But not this time it seemed, as he had a positive response for once!

"What are we waiting for?" Dale blurted out. True. For all the available seats in the bus had been taken up. Dale's grimaced face did the remaining part of the talking and the driver appeared to understand him well enough.

"Sorry!" The driver spoke apologetically - rather unusual of the normally impolite bus drivers who plied this route. He continued: "We left our spare tyre at the vulcaniser's last night. But not to worry, they are bringing it shortly". But Dale was not impressed.

"You silly man! Didn't you know you had to do that before now? Or does a farmer go farming without his hoe and other implements?" Dale's rude retort made nearly everyone wonder if he had a previous personal axe to grind with the driver who he went on to further describe as "a careless and forgetful moron".

Luckily the tyre soon arrived and the journey commenced. The last hour was like sunbathing in an oven. Dale's own case was made worse because he was was 'dressed to kill' in his three-piece suit on a thirty-degree-plus afternoon. Fair enough, he like

'Femi Abidogun

every other candidate had been advised to come "appropriately dressed" in his interview invitation letter and of course to come with "all relevant certificates".

Thanks to the driver's Formula One like driving skills, they arrived in the big city in less than the normal two hours it usually took. The roadside traders welcomed the bus into the city with their numerous products ranging from smelly fried snacks to electronics from the Far East. The newspaper vendors were not left out of the scramble and Dale decided to have a look at the dailies just in case he was asked during the interview about current 'topical' issues.

Most of the headlines such as the disgrace of a local politician and the impending royal visit were by now stale news to Dale as he had kept a vigil with his radio all night. However, before he turned his face away from the newspapers he let out a shrill scream. He had just noticed a newspaper headline which said something about certificates and subsequently this had reminded him of his own certificates.

"Oh no! I didn't remember to bring along my certificates". He continued to cry hysterically almost bursting everyone's eardrums. He wondered if this was fate's revenge on him for his choice of words to the driver. Some of the other passengers consoled him while a few others including the driver and his assistant giggled away.

"Tell me, boss" asked the driver's assistant in low tones, facing the driver who was still giggling: "What kind of farmer goes to his farm without his hoe?"

The bus driver responded loudly to everyone's hearing: "A silly one, in fact a silly, careless and forgetful moron!".

Jude Ashworth

My career started in managing clinical waste thence the Tidy Britain Group, becoming the Regional Director for the West Midlands. I qualified as a clinical aromatherapist and Reiki Master, opening my own practice.

My love of poetry writing was inspired by my photographs. Then my writing progressed to include short stories, plays and monologues. But my first love is poetry, some based on a canal walking journey from Spaghetti Junction to Gas Street Basin. These were exhibited in a British Waterways exhibition at Cox's Wharf in Stratford upon Avon and then at Angel's Pop Up Gallery in New Street.

To my joy in Remembrance week I had a poem chosen for Poet's Corner in the Sutton Observer, under my pen name Jude Ashworth.

I enjoy giving public readings of my poems and am a regular performer at Poetry Bites at the Kitchen Garden Café in Kings Heath.

I joined the Pens creative writing group at Erdington Library in 2012. Jan Watts (former Birmingham Poet Laureate) who was the facilitator asked me to take over the group which I did in January 2013. Encouragement is given to all sorts of genres of creative writing.

Wishing to widen my involvement in creative writing I joined Writers Without Borders a few years ago , a wonderfully diverse group. They inspire me as their brilliant writings are very evocative. Also there is a wide variety of opportunities to become involved in performing your creative words.

City of Strife

He stepped on her face smudging the lines.
Another spat, spittle trickled down her chin.
Children stamped their feet crushing eye and nose.
Dogs defecated, which was spread far and wide.

A burger left its greasy trail over forehead and hair
trampled beyond recognition with detritus and city living,
surviving just, but now almost obliterated.
Gone the chiseled features of a glamorous woman.

The heavens in their torment raged with thunder
the tears of the sky created a deluge,
at lightning speed filling the gutters,
blocking grey slithering roads of escape.
First one foot then another repeating
till life was choked out of her city folk.

Challenging generations as breath induced breath
stretched to the limit bodies broken on racks
Viewed in sensuous clarity corpses giving way
choking on fumes, the glamour woman breathed her last.

To open is to receive and to receive is a gift.

Each gift is a treasure and that is YOU.

Just Pebbles

The sucking and slaking of pebbles,
Shushing and shagging the beach.
Surf pounding to the pull and push.
Life journeying never ending, grinding,
commuting, circling quintessence of
thought, living and forever changing,
lulling the mind of the unforgiving.
Pebbles of life that we all are,
Mind-bending rituals never ceasing.
Somnolent face turned to the sun.
Curlicue in thought never binding,
releasing riches beyond, culminating
in elegant stature and life styling.
But still the slaking and shagging
of those pebbles on the beach ....

To dream is to be alive in an illusion
To be is to live in the now.
But to live your dreams gives a touch of magic
And brings life to an illusion.

Roof Scapes

I dance across the rooftops
and listen to the wind,
put my ear to the chimneys
and hear them whispering,
whispering about the chimney sweeps
and their sooty girls and boys.

Slipping and sliding across the roofs
a woosh and whistling is heard.
Looking to the moon that hangs high
a spiral of spirits on the wind float by.
They come to rest on a slated roof
their little bare feet cold and blue.
Hand in hand they slowly dance
along to the beat of the wind.
Little boys twisted and bent
tiny girls all dirty and black,
black with soot that choked.
But Angels are espied,
gathering up, embracing all,
taking them to their hearts
each one of their sooty little souls.

Tiptoeing on the tiles
sliding on the rooftops
peeping into skylights.......

Patricia Bamurangirwa

My name is Patricia Bamurangirwa. I was born in Rwanda in 1949, now resident in West Midlands Britain.

As many African girls at the time, I missed higher education among other opportunities, but refused to allow that limitation of education to tie me back.

Most of all I wanted to be a good example to other women to have full confidence in themselves and know that they can achieve.

After this I had to go through many difficulties because I was a girl, among other reasons, but now I am with a group of poetry people, Writers Without Borders.

I am the author of three books now. My first book, 'Rwanda Yesterday', is about the history of my country Rwanda.

The second, 'My Mother's Dreams', which is the story of my life, was selected in the best books category in February 2015 by Books Monthly.

Finally, 'Patriotism', which is a collection of my poems.

Time to break the laws

They realized that now there was a baby on the way and since they couldn't know how long Maria would take to get proper legal papers to settle as a British citizen, and with the huge expenses that come with a new born baby, Sandra and husband suggested that when the baby was born, the baby was to be registered as John's under his surname, so that it would be easy for both of them, because in that way the baby would get the same benefits as any other British baby which would help Maria to take care of the baby as she prepared for her next step of looking for a job, at the same time it would help them reduce expenses for the baby. Note that, to outsiders, it would be strange how Sandra could take in John's girlfriend under the same roof. They also tried to talk to one of their friends to give Maria papers so that she could work under her name since any grown-up person needs pocket money and they could not tell how long the papers would take

They were good people who had many good friends so it was not hard for them to get a favour from any of them. That request also was not strange to many, it was common among many of them, with different goals and ideals and if they got people to assist them with their papers in that case they would drop their true identities and work under a false identity. Now Maria was expecting her baby and she had a job, step by step she came to meet different people and some of them from back home. Among the people she met she made friends. Some of her friends were those kinds of people who believed they knew everything. And they briefed her about the country she was in, how Britain cares about women and children that she was lucky to get a baby when she was there, because after having a baby that it would automatically be the Queen's child and would not be forced out of the country, nor would the mother.

They advised her that to make things easier for her and maybe make quick riches, since the father of her child was not her husband and the family had everything, she could be clever and get some of their

Time to break the laws

property in a simple way and get the legal papers she needed, even a full passport, just after getting the baby she could move to any of her friends and then make up fake stories and they assured her of their assistance in that matter. They persuaded her to go to a family court and report John and his wife accusing them of abuse and torture.

Maria immediately bought the idea, the only way to make quick riches in Britain. She was excited and she couldn't wait for that time. When she was home talking to any family member, either John or Sandra or any of the children, she pretended to be part of the family but deep inside her mind she was thinking how foolish they are to think that she cannot get any other means of acquiring part of their wealth! She knew that she was sitting on a time bomb which would burst anytime. After delivering the baby she would find a reason to move to one of the family friends and John and the whole family had no problem with that.

The time came when she went to the police and reported that what forced her out of John's place was abuse and torture. She reported that she had been under intense abuse and torture from the family ever since she started living with John's family. She added that John was threatening her friends who were putting her up in their house, she added that she came on John's invitation who promised to get her a job but later went back on every promise made to her.

When she was asked what kind of abuse she got when she was in John's family she reported many different horrible events: like rape, work as a house girl for no pay, poor accommodation.... which was a very serious case then.

Now it turned out to be a big case which needed court intervention. The judge asked both sides to bring proof of what they were saying or witnesses. When John's neighbours heard those stories they were very surprised and Sandra asked John what kind of family he had

Patricia Bamurangirwa

back home. This shocked John as well and made him not only angry but he was ashamed too. When the stories reached back home, most of them were shocked and ashamed and they regretted sending her there. Most of the people who Maria expected to support her in her case against John, when the time came they realised that the case couldn't go any further and they dropped out of it. It was now John's family back home which received the shocking news about Maria's behaviour; they thought that this could not have been done to John and his family given their sacrifices in helping relatives. They expected Maria to change her behaviour which included greed once she reached Britain.

Back home Maria was known to be greedy, she had been charged with a criminal offence. Much as the family was trying hard to keep it a secret and protect her, she was finally arrested and imprisoned for some time. Later one of the friends who knew Maria from back home told John the whole truth about Maria's true character. A friend went as far as advising John to make research back home about her previous offences so that he could get evidence in his defence. This forced John to go back home and get evidence to defend himself from a girl who was determined to destroy his family and snatch his wealth just because he was generous to her!

What surprised all who knew about that case was the one person who supported Maria was her mother! The mother also expected to get quick riches from John, but she couldn't do more to help her daughter.

The evidence John got from back home helped him and in the end they deported Maria back home with her baby.

Now John is wondering if tomorrow he will ever help anyone again.

(This is a true story but all names have been changed.)

Rashida Begum

I enjoy writing poetry and stories. They allow me to express myself. I have been writing for a few years but have been an avid reader since I was a teenager.

Midnight Cat

The blinding mask of day
Ambushed by the gathering darkness
Half light
Succumbs to Indian inkiness
Secret smile of pale translucence
Vanishes as
The midnight march crowds
Into blackout
Gagging the moon
The midnight cat
Prowls
Pricking the eternal hush
Of graveyard bodies
The slow stealth of the sabre-toothed
Beast
Stealing across the
Cavernous chasm

Lost

Laughter has been hunted to near extinction. It is a rare bird that was sighted a decade ago in this particular household. Bitterness crept into the corners anchoring her mouth and the lips clamped shut against the world then her eyes died when he left. The soft sensual mouth became a washing line tethered to her daughter. Only her skin revived and each day she sat holding a mirror up to herself looking for clues to her identity. Who was she? She felt like an imposter. Only her daughter's imploring eyes stopped her from walking out on herself. The make-up hid the truth. Everyone was bewitched by the beautiful face. Only she saw the ugliness as she washed her 'face' away each day.

Mother & Son

Getting out of bed as daylight
pokes its unwelcome head around
the door
as a mountain of exhaustion slams
your inert body against the soft
warmth of the feathery
cocoon
it lulls you into a deep sea
of sleep
your little son clings limpet-like
his limbs entwined in yours
mother & son lying entangled
like a golden starfish
submerged in slumber

Broken

A haghand crouching crablike

Bones protruding pathetically
                        pokey fingers askew

Stabbing the sodden Earth

A sinister stillness grows
               sudden scurrying sends it
                             shooting forwards

The ripe skin of the blossoming mushroom
                                       upended

Denuded by the pounding pain of the incessant rain

Twisted
        mangled by the roadside

Abandoned by its owner
                lies the broken umbrella

Art Gallery Photo

An abandoned air

Hangs over the dilapidated desk

His hungry mouth gaping

Open

Completely broken

As they violently wrenched tools

From the bowels of his womb

Desperate silence reigns

Arrogant in his triumph

As the phone sits still strangled on its cord

It will never ring again

Disembodied voices whisper

After dark

Echoing their disquiet

Sue Brown

Creative Writer and Poet

My poetry, my writing I guess, is to know, to share, to perpetuate my notions, my feelings, brought forward from the creative consciousness into breath into matter!

Over the years, I have been involved with various creative projects across different art forms. I've encouraged the production of visual art and creative writing in response to different experiences, including collaborations with musicians and theatre, radio and TV. I've also been involved extensively in educational work within schools, including projects for Birmingham's Writing West Midlands

Since 2001 I have been a member of one of Birmingham's largest writers group *Writers without Borders* (WWB) and have been its figurehead since 2008. I've enjoyed interesting and inspiring moments with the group and love the way we are working and developing together to make WWB what it is today.

I thank WWB for trusting me and allowing me to be part of their experience!

My Epigrams*

A **democracy**
demonstrates controlled options
pitched as **freedom of choice**

By design, **Freedom
of Expression** can be repressed by
man's freedom of speech

Man's Freedom of Speech
is enforced by laws sanctioned
to control purpose

When **oppression's** in
the game, **freedom** will always
be last in the race

*A short poem, having a witty, satirical, or ingenious ending

Black Beauty

Beauty it is said is in the eye of the beholder...

Look and acknowledge the blackness of the beginning
See and know beauty from which all came

Look and acknowledge the blackness of the heavens
See and know beauty, infinity jewelled with stars majestic

Look and acknowledge the blackness of the deep
See and know beauty, life not seen on land

Look and acknowledge the blackness of the rich soil
See and know beauty, sustenance sustaining all

Look and acknowledge the blackness of the womb
See and know beauty, perfection for all human conception

Look and acknowledge the blackness of an Afrikan
See and know beauty in Creation!

Out of blackness came light
Without blackness, there is no light!

My poem is called Poetry

While sipping on a memory I discovered within myself
the ability to work to yield to engage my thoughts
my words
    my pen…
       to sound
          to voice
to listen to dare
to write to remember…my reasons my direction

While sipping on a memory I re-discovered the *me*
within myself
       to know to share
          to perpetuate…
              my notions my feelings
                  brought forward from the creative consciousness
                    into breath into matter!

While sipping on a memory I discovered
within myself creativity in style, and form evoked as
    Poetry!
      Words of imagery sketched using the wand of vibrations
inspired by dynamic rhythmic chants
       Poetry!
         Words formed outside the norm of customary conversation
and moods
narratives ingeniously joining lettering resourcefully
          Poetry!
            Words disseminated within the melanin-vital ink
enabling blank pages and performance spaces to converse its
dialogue of
              Poetry!
                Words reflecting and remembering the past
future etched within the oral traditions by offering my words and
contribution to the walls and lining of this great universe…..

                    Poetry!

My love is Irie

Here I go again
taking the journey of love again
dancing to the steps of joy again
grooving to the intimacy of two again

all in the name of love again

I recognise myself for who I am again
I feel safe to allow myself to be me again
I know strength when I see it within me again

I'm ready to give
to receive
to be
me
in love again

Here I go again
taking the journey of love again
dancing to the steps of joy again
grooving to the intimacy of two again
all in the name of love again

I know how to whisper words of love again
I know how to dream dreams of being in love again
once again
I'll surrender to overpowering feelings of fearlessness in love again
all because of you I'm in love again
and yes I am reminded of how to love myself again

Here I go again
taking the journey of love again
dancing to the steps of joy again
grooving to the intimacy of two again
all in the name of love again
my love is Irie!

Keisha Diamond

I am an artist and I love expressing myself through a variety of forms including poetry, photography, dance, painting, music and performance.
I am inspired by nature, life, spirituality and truth as well as exploring many emotions we experience.
Passionate about legacy and empowerment, when collating these poems I asked myself, what do I want to share with the world? This is the inspiration that came... Enjoy.

Found My NYC
I Found My New York in the streets of Birmingham
On the banks of the canal with reflections of Venice
In high rise buildings and prestige of the Mailbox
In glittering skylines and horizontal depths, a sea of sparkles
Magical views from the 25th floor, heart bursting and eyes soaring
Experiencing the old time cottage cafe
Admiring cobweb decors, trinkets and blazing fires
Celebrating all there is to be celebrated with a hot choc, cream and flake
Apple, cranberry and lemon
In a beautiful mirror with hearty company
I Found My New York,
My Adventure...
My Music...
My World...
Within Me.
In the streets of Birmingham.

I See You

I see your beauty

I see your power

I see your resilience

I see your transformation

I see your style

I see your elegance

I see your wisdom

I see your fruitfulness

I see your determination

I see your perseverance

I see your kindness

I see your generosity

I see your willingness

I see your expansion

I see your truth

I see you.

Truly Transforming

I am truly transforming
  from a busy bzzzzzzzzzzzzzzzzzzzzzzz!
  - into a seamingless Butterfly

From concrete jungles
  to mountain tops, where Fresh air Rises
    Heats and Cools

Water falls Beneath my Feet
Serenity Greens Envelope
in a curvature of arms

Where ☺ says More
  than any words
    possibly could

I am Truly Transforming
into a Goddess of Wisdom
Beauty & Light

Where the whims & whizzes of other people
  upon me have no plight

Keisha Diamond

Where laughter and gurgles
Have so much more meaning
and in the depths of my womb, the Nature of Creation,
I am Birthing

Where easy sleep
Brings the Mind to Rest ...

Yet Excitable in the Flourishing
Visions of Colour
Astro Travels & Discovering Whole New Worlds Anew!

Where Morning Brings Enlightenment
In the Stillness

Where 'Mistakes' & Labels have no form,
Transmuted in Higher Learnings
And endless Possibilities ...

Where LOVE Reigns Supreme

I am Truly Transforming

Predencia Dixon

I joined Writers Without Borders (WWB) in 2006, the same year I was introduced to performance poetry. WWB has provided many opportunities for me to showcase my poetry to a wide variety of audiences, and in 2011 I published a small anthology and a CD of my poems, both entitled Raw.

In 2012 I decided to try my hand at writing stories and have now published two novels and two books of short stories. One book *Love is Not a Reward* is accompanied by a workbook for parents.

My writing is mainly concerned with people's intimate experiences of social and political issues.

Publications :

Raw Vols 1 and 2 (2011) Cymbals Publishing

Raw CD (2011) Cymbals Publishing

Dare to Love (2012) Matador (As Penny Dixon)

Betrayed (2012) Matador (As Penny Dixon)

Never on Sunday (2013) Createspace (As Penny Dixon)

Love is Not a Reward (2014) Createspace

Love is Not a Reward Workbook (2014) Createspace

Caribbean Cowboy

The crabs running round like headless chickens. If you don't know the beach you'll miss them. They the same colour as the sand, pale yellow with little flecks of whatever the sea throw up that day. They digging deep, throwing out sand from way down the hole. A sure sign there's a storm coming. I look down the beach, sun bouncing off it like disco lights off a wall. People still sunbathing, still playing volleyball, still trying to make a date. I turn my head to check another crab hole. That's when I see it, barely sticking out the sand like it shy, don't want to expose itself. I ease it out gently and give it a home on my palm. A diamond teardrop earring. Intact with backing clip. I carefully wipe off the sand and drop it in my shirt pocket. I'll try it on later.

The wind picking up speed, people trying to stop their things blowing away, another half hour and they'll give up, go back to their cars, their hotels, their houses. I check the trees. They swaying like they in some slow waltz. Soon they'll be bowing and curtseying; branches tipping the sand, straightening up to start again. Time to leave. I stand up, stretch out my long legs. People will be staying in tonight, only ghosts and emergency services on the streets tonight. I stop by the supermarket. Pick up tinned fish, bread, candles, batteries and bottle of Appleton Special. It could be a long night.

By five o'clock the storm hit. Rain like horse hoofs on the roof, scratching like demented souls at the windows. Wind matching it with angry howls; like it and the ghosts having a dispute. Trees everywhere join the dance, some bend further than others. Some fall over trying to compete with their more flexible neighbours.

Tonight I can dress up in safety. Nobody going to disturb me tonight. I get the case down from the top of the wardrobe, lay my clothes out on the bed, rub each piece against my face, inhale

Caribbean Cowboy

the perfume. I shower, rub Ylang Ylang essential oil into every pore; then I begin. Always the same order. Red thong, red padded brassiere, yellow silk pants, red silk blouse tied under my brassiere, red stilettos and finally the cowboy hat, drawstring under my chin. When I finish I look in the mirror.

I'm a vision of beauty. Always. I smooth my hand over my blouse, my waist, my hips. I turn this way, that way, admire myself all ways. That's when I remember the earring. It's perfect, made for me; don't even need its twin as I only have one ear pierced.

I'm so busy I don't notice that the wind get under the roof till it give one big push and lift it clean off. Everything start flying around, whacking my head, my chest, my back, slapping my arms, my legs. I know how dangerous this is. I have to run before the walls fall in and crush me to death.

I kick off the stilettos and run barefoot down the street, wind chasing me, rain lashing me, trees threatening to fall on me. I'm six foot, more legs than chest and tonight I need them. I see a house with a light on. I pound on the door in time with the pounding in my chest. A big round man open it a little crack, in case the wind blow it wide open. He look like he's about to shut it again on me. I put my foot in the way and beg him. 'Please I need shelter.'

I'm in a room with five other men, all of them look drunk, lots of empty bottles of Appleton. They pointing and laughing and calling me batty man. That's when I remember my clothes. One of them notice my earring.

'Is that real diamond batty man?'

No words come out my mouth when I open it. I nod.

Predencia Dixon

'I want it.' His eyes are red and narrow.

My hand fly to my ear, the only part of me I feel can protect.

'Hold him boys!'

Before I can move four of them on me, rum on their breath hate in their hearts. I'm face down on the floor earring side up. Instinct says fight but can't move, they on every place that could move.

I feel fire in my ear, pain like all the devils of hell let loose on my ear. I hear the big man laugh. Think I hear him say 'Thank you batty man.'

There's another pain in my ear, stinging, like salt or vinegar or...

'Have some lime to keep it fresh.'

Then they're off me. My hand go to my ear, feel the thickening blood, smell it in the room, feel the space where my ear lobe used to be. I can't look at them, too frightened.

'Get out of here batty man before I cut off something else,' him threaten me.

I instinctively know where the door is. Nobody try to stop me. The wind sound different in that ear. I run and run and run till I find myself back at the beach. I know a little place under the rock. I crawl in there, share it with the crabs.

Later, the hospital say I must report it to the police. I don't tell them the fat man with my earring is the police reception officer.

Inge Durrani

Words have always come easily to me, having been brought up in several different countries and lived in a variety of cities around the world. The first time I felt the urge to express myself in the form of poetry was in the early 1970s when there was much talk about Nelson Mandela and I had many curious questions about his life, e.g. what he looked like and why he was imprisoned. Then, as a young teacher, I met a colleague who admitted she wrote poetry. That was a real inspiration to me. Words have been meaningful to me because of the different aspects of their origin, syntax and semantics, and also for their power for good or evil. After my retirement in 2000, I bought a book on how to write poetry, etc. – much to the disgust of some poets I know.

Then through talking to a member of Writers Without Borders I realized that many bound-up feelings can be put into poetic form and can bring release. Thanks to everyone there who encouraged me so generously.

Heimat

The time: soon after the war, a joyful spring day morning.
The place: no longer a house, but a home in the West.
The people: a skinny young woman on a wooden bench in an
    attic room facing north;
two hungry little girls snuggling in her arms.
No fairy story on her knees,
but the girls listening to the unimaginable beauty
the woman's words create now in their minds.

The woman sings with a low voice a series of her native tunes
    some in German, some in Polish.
The children do not know yet
that they will never see that homeland again;
that they will never want – for fear – their mother's Heimat.

The woman has been aware for quite some time
that her beloved homeland is expunged already from the map;
recalls the stark endurance of Vertriebensein, of expulsion;
and can only dream of her Silesia.

Schlesien, my beauty!
Where are my forests, mountains and rivers;
my large family, husband, father to the girls
whom they will never meet again?
Gone forever.

Schlesien, my proud one!
Your mask is off and after many years
the wounds will be healed again,
and culture, flowers, friends and families
will then exist once more.

Schlesien, my love!
I kiss your fear of death to teach me
to dance again and embrace a new life.

A New Life

Will I remember cradling in my mother's womb pulsing
with love and strength, and I
often being jostled and shoved.

Will I remember my mother's singing voice and
the many azans that calmed her,
when they still had a happy home in Sure –
even though half-collapsed and pock-marked by bullets.

Will I remember the trembling and shaking and stabbing
I felt when my mother was told –
about my father's death.

Will I remember my older brothers' and sisters'
anguished screams and cries then.
Will I remember how small my space became
when my mother hobbled across the mountains to safety,
exhausted and bewildered;
when my siblings leaned into her at night to rest
constricting me even further.

Will I remember the groans my mother groaned
dragging herself through the cold and rain
with despair from which her spirit might not recover.

I will remember, though,
how eager I was to see and smell and taste
this glorious and jubilant world.

Untitled

Proud men are coming to attack me;
cruel men are trying to kill me –
men who do not care about God (Psalm 54:3)

Have I tried to understand their actions,
mistaken their behaviour towards my self?
Have I just seen the situations
as my small mind can comprehend?

You have rescued me from all my troubles,
and I have seen my enemies defeated (Psalm 54:7)

Rescued I am when I believe
in that great strength you have endowed me with.
Rescued I am when I forgive
all those invisible, imaginary foes.

Wake up, my soul!
Wake up, my harp and lyre!
I will wake up the sun (Psalm 57:8)

Each morn of mine is like a pearl –
each one is strung together
to make my chain of life.

Ita Gooden

I am Ita Gooden aka Miss Culture Jam and I also write under the name of C J Lewis. I am a qualified midwife and nurse specialist in Sexual Health with a BA in Business Administration. I have also lectured at Birmingham City University.

Currently I live in Birmingham and am now a writer and performance poet who was one of the twelve poets chosen to write a poem for the London 2012 Olympic and Paralympic games; the poem entitled 'Breathe' has been viewed by millions online and in the Olympic Park.

My first collection of poems is on a CD with accompanying music entitled 'La Fire' which can be found in a number of libraries in the UK. My most recent publication is a book of poetry entitled 'On the face of it'.

Moonlight

The moon is shining bright
Trees glistened from its bathing light
What great delight!

Oh beautiful moonlight
You are a magnificent sight
Enhancing everything in your path
You are at the heart of many lovers' dreams
As they stride hand in hand in lovers' land
Your beams penetrating deep in their inner beings

Your shining light bright or dim
Breaking through clouds thick or thin
In starry skies universally you shine
On the grass wet with dew
On the trees and across the lake
There is no mistake that, like the wind blows
Where it pleases, your light beams with tranquillity
Oozes with personality and ability.

The continuous change to your size and shape
Causes many a debate
Sometimes you are full-bodied
At other times you are half with a different shape.
Entwined with the sun expressing your magical skills
An eclipse is the result when you kiss.

Oh beautiful one your creation is everything magical
Your presence enchanting for many precious moments
Factual or mythical.
From whence you came and where you go
Will always be part of nature's show.

Window to the Soul

I looked into his eyes and was transfixed by what
I saw or could not see.
The clean area or sclera as it's called,
so dense even tense,
not giving anything away.
As he blinked the area appeared pink,
I continued to think.

My gaze fixed and focussed on
the centre of his eyes.
The darkest brown you ever did see,
all shiny and glazed,
he looked dazed.
The pupils of his eyes made contact
with mine,
they were ready to dine.

Fixation and enlargement,
I was transported and elevated
to another level.
His eyes were no longer a window
but an open door.

Inviting, enticing and exciting,
pupils entwined and searching
for the soul.
This is the right mould.

Soulmates we became
a date was made
yet no words were spoken.
Our eyes were fixed to the prize.
A window to the soul,
Love.
Come and dine
till the end of time.
A window to the soul, the soul, the soul.

Revenge

My man Dan, he was my greatest fan
I would say up to the other day.

Upon him all my love I had bestowed
No holds barred at any time he could
Mark my card.

So to hear our friend say
That with this wench he did stay
For a whole night and a day
For me sheer dismay.

The first thought that entered my head
Was to knock him dead
Until my friend said
A Bobbitt would be
More deserving and the wench
Could have it as a serving
For a starter, main course
Or dessert as this was sure to hurt.

Dan my ex man now lacks the urge
And desire to flirt
With a skirt or shirt.

Nabila Jameel

I am a Manchester based poet, of Pakistani origin, born and bred in the UK. My poems have been published by Commonword, Stand magazine, the Poetry Review and Bloodaxe (recent anthology 'Out of Bounds'). I was runner up in the 2010 Manchester Cathedral International Religious Poetry Competition with my poem 'The Last Prayer'.

After the Explosion

    Severed limbs, still marked
    with honeymoon kisses,
    re-attach with rough seams.
    She gives herself a new blood supply.

    Like a corpse revived
    or a post-stroke patient
    or a traumatised soldier
    she learns to speak and walk again.

Father in Gaza

Your home to which you return
Is now a tower block of blown-out

eye sockets, nightmarish, stooping
over the vast field of concrete,

bleeding the voices of children
who once held these hands.

Hands now clearing rubble, brick, bone,
teeth and toys. Dolls with missing limbs,

and bullet-holed belly buttons,
their faces grey with grime, dust, ash and blood.

A father rescues a doll's face to reveal
a plastic smile mimicking his own.

Back Yard

Every summer
on a Saturday morning
you bathed us in the back yard
of our tiny terraced house.

We had pink Lux, a bucket, a sponge and a jug.
The sun would dry the suds on our skin
that would stick like glue and make us white.
Bubbles were bigger than our house.

You rinsed us and then we were brown again.
We sat towel wrapped in the sun
and shivered while droplets fell onto our flip flops.
Smiles were bigger than our house.

A Book Closer to Home

Every Saturday mum took us to the library.
We dispersed into different parts of the room,

craving this yellow smell of bound paper
and a peep into lives we did not live -
where tea was not chai, but dinner.

Mum sat in the Urdu section,
soon dissolving into a magazine
full of squiggles that only made sense to her.

Her large almond eyes smiled.
Her soft fingers turned the pages,
pausing while she glanced at us with motherly duty.

We sat with our books on the carpeted floor,
following the curves and lines of English
with our fingertips,

the red signs on the mahogany shelves
silencing our tongues.

Tessa Kate Lowe

I had been writing a form of poetry for years when I discovered the joys of WWB. Suddenly I find myself writing a form of prose. Who knows where that might lead?

Calling

I was put on this earth to write short stories and make people happy. This was something I had never realised until my neighbour Don told me just before my sixty-ninth birthday.

I wasn't interested in writing short stories but have always been rather too interested in making people happy. I had been trying constantly up until that moment to do just that and I ought to have been a bit better at it by then.

I was not. I was something of a continuous and continuing abject failure at making people happy. This is not really surprising as no-one can make someone else happy or unhappy if you think about it.

Happiness lies within and comes from your core or your attitude of mind. I spent most of my life forgetting that fact and made myself very unhappy indeed when people were not made happy by me.

I also spent a lot of time making myself unhappy over the years by wondering what I was supposed to be doing here. What was my purpose ?

I believed I might be happy once I had the answer to that question and now I had. My neighbour Don had given it to me.

"You were put on this earth to write short stories " he told me emphatically.

When I tried to argue that I had no intention of writing short stories

Calling

he repeated himself. "You were put on this earth to write short stories," and here he paused, "and so make people happy ".

He is cunning is Don. That was a clever bait he used and before I knew it I was hooked.

Let me tell you a story. Perhaps it will make you happy. Perhaps it won't. That all depends on you.

Once upon a time, it wasn't in your time, it wasn't in my time but it was in somebody's time, a sailor sailed the seas.

He had been born and brought up to be a farmer like his father and his father's father before him. The farm he lived on was full of sheep. From a very early age he was taught to take his sheep up onto the hills with his dog Janie. He learned to count by counting sheep.

Counting sheep was a very responsible and important job and the boy was proud to be doing it. It made him feel like a man. A man like his his father, his father's father and his father's father before him.

The name of the boy was Jack. He had been named Jack after his father. Jacks had farmed the land and counted sheep and tended lambs in springtime and had shorn sheep in summer for as long as anyone who knew those hills had been aware. Jacks were part of the landscape. They were part of the hills and dales as much as the rising sun and the setting moon.

Suddenly one morning it was as if the sun had failed to rise from its bed behind the hills. Jack ate his breakfast of bread and cheese quite as on any other ordinary morning. Then he put on his hat, picked up a small bundle and said goodbye.

"Goodbye ", he said. "Goodbye mother. Goodbye father. Goodbye dog. I am going to sail the seas."

Jack's mother's chin fell down to her neck and her mouth gaped wide open. Jack's father's chin fell down and his mouth gaped wide open too. This always happened when they were surprised but Jack had

Calling

never seen it before. Nothing much surprising had ever happened in the twenty years he had been shepherding sheep. Jack didn't see it even then, for his back was to his parents as he said goodbye and he never stopped to wave.

He walked and he walked and he walked. He had no idea where to find the sea. He had never been further than the hills and there was no sign of it from the top. He had no real idea of what the sea looked like.

Grass, he knew; sheep, he knew. He loved the grass and the hills and the sheep but the idea of the sea had sprung up in him full-born just the night before. He woke up certain as to what he had been born for. He had been born to be a sailor and to sail the seas.

Here we find him, out on the vast ocean, alone and a-sail, in a small boat that someone had given him. The owner had suddenly decided that after a lifetime of fishing, he had had enough. He had no use for his boat any longer.

Jack had come upon the sea after three full days of tireless walking. His heart was steady and his soul was singing with the certainty that he would find what he was looking for, for it was where he was meant to be.

He was tired, footsore and hungry when he came to a little fishing village. There were about twenty small white cottages, a shop and a local hostelry and there were boats bobbing all about on calm blue water at the end of day.

Jack went into the inn. He had little money but he had some skeins of finest sheepswool that he had packed in his bag. He asked if the innkeeper would accept one in exchange for a sup of ale and a hunk of bread and cheese.

It was fortunate for Jack that the innkeeper's wife had been nagging him incessantly to give her money to get some wool. Times were hard for everyone in those days and he was sad not to be able to afford to get her what she wanted. His wife might be a nag but they had been

Tessa Kate Lowe

---

married for a long time and he was used to it. The innkeeper loved his wife and would do whatever he could to make her happy.

A skein of wool would make her very happy indeed so he gladly took it and gave Jack his ale and food.

There was only one other man sitting at the counter supping his ale. He was obviously a fisherman. He was also obviously quite a drunk fisherman and was loudly singing a shanty. The chorus was easy to learn and Jack started singing it along with him.

The two men began conversing in the friendliest of fashions and Jack soon learned that the fisherman whose name was Jim was not happy. If he had no boat to worry about he could get on with finding out what he was supposed to be doing on this earth. This was the question that had started bothering him suddenly in the past month. He had lost concentration and had lost heart and his catch became smaller and smaller each day.

Jack kindly offered to take the boat off his hands for him and promised to look after it well. The fisherman was pleased.

Jack never promised that he would bring it back to prove how well he had looked after it and the man never asked him to. He just ordered another glass of ale and his singing became louder and more carefree than you could ever imagine.

The next morning the former fisherman came to show Jack the ropes. He showed him how the sails worked. He showed him where the oars were in case the wind died down. He taught him to tie a sailor's knot or two and had then taught him all he knew so off Jack set.

Jim was soon a mere dancing dot on the horizon, his shanty singing on the wind. There is no place here to set down what became of him or what he decided to do. For all we know he might be dancing still.

Jack, however, had found his element. Away away on the briny sea he sailed, discovering what he was born to do.

Ahmed Magare

I am an interdisciplinary artist, poet and writer. I am originally from Somalia. Having migrated with my family to the Netherlands when I was three years of age I lived with my family in the Netherlands for most of my life – and eventually decided to live in England to pursue my further education in creative arts.

In my writing I explore the notions of 'hyper-dislocation', 'suicidal confessions' and my experience living in the West through a poetic and static lens of self-reflection and self-perseverance. I navigate between the notions of 'longing' and 'belonging' – and comment on social-political and cultural subjects inhabiting the space of global Somalis.

To Catch a Sailing Boat

To catch a sailing boat. To fish for a mighty dream. I understand, my Hooyo, when you hide your everything in silence. Let me find it with you. May it be loud or seem impossible. Let us find it, together, in time – we cherish. I understand, my mother, but I will never fully understand your mysterious courageous ways. Do I really need to tell you all that I have inside? And all the things that I want to do for you? I'm sure you feel it. Inside. Sometimes, I'm weak, stubborn and I feel incomplete. I feel like falling, falling outside the realms of time. I know you have held this weight for too long. Maybe I'm wrong. Don't cry mother. I am but a blink of breath that is passing by. A crying breeze, when I massage your ageing feet. I try to recover times that you sacrificed yourself, for me. I am a longing wave that is everlasting; belonging underneath your feet lies perfection. "Everlasting-Eden". May I grasp for life that is never lasting? She says: "you will know this, my son, when death has come close, to call, scratching on the surface of your skin, in between us lies unconditional love." I remember, my body being fragile, and the severe symptoms of internal panic, festering errors of my past. It hurts, and haunts me more, even when I think of it. I will feel it more when my spirit sinks low, faded, limbs of shattered hopes. Oh mother, I will carelessly sing and dwell in your gold. I am just a wind that is following, running to catch a sailing boat. To catch a sailing boat! To catch a sailing boat!

I am but a sound, a name, and a vulnerable flesh – dying to give back to those who deserve me in my emptiness. With foolish love, I wonder, steady-down my struggling kind – I was bound to explore the universe with you. I guess I never knew all along that my universe was you. Shining from within.

Words

My words are born
I am born in a chaotic brain
Explosive thoughts, written on a silent night
Calm my mind, catch every second, express every emotion through words that scratch more than just the surface
I am still dreaming of what the earth will bring forth
In tsunami storms, we swim

Think!
My words will need some oxygen, to survive because every form of hate we consume is poison!
So let the heart bleed seven wishes
Roll your boat, roll your boat
For more hope will bring you gently down the street
Life is just a dream, a test to be
So treasure the beauty of simplicity!
And let your mind rest in this comfortable oasis, private, spacious, abundantly amazing terrarium
you call "home"
My words are born...

Born far away from home

But as soon we put the first leg out in reality, we are prepared to be consumed by the flames of the universe
The songs of welcoming birds, parading school kids and cries of sleepless drunks meditating in the morning daylight

Ahmed Magare

Every word has a story

Every story has a word

The earth has become an open platform of swollen talent and undeniable expression, but you can't hide!
Every blind word will expose your deepest thoughts and desires
- so live! And smell the vibrating air!
You are soon to be followed by our words,
because words are not just words
Words are like shadows,
a character of home

Barbara Peterson

I've been lucky with my family--we are 9 now. Even at a young age they let me travel and write, enduring our living in clutter. They're all able to write from the heart, (one's a journalist) and are so adventurous they take my breath away.

After collecting music in Sierra Leone and doing an MA here in African Studies, I had the chance to go to Nigeria to meet popular praise-singers. I saw how they shaped public opinion about the rich and powerful, where their biting humour won them public affection. Back in the UK I've worked and taught while writing poetry and plays, many about Africa. I've enjoyed seeing many pieces performed and published, also sharing light-hearted poems with audiences who enjoy a laugh.

That Wonderful Somebody - Nigeria, 1973

That's how their singer, Shata, was known by Nigerians, who claimed Allah had given him 'a windpipe made of diamonds'. Who else could sing for 7 hours? Who else improvised with such wit? Come for a night to any humble club and, if the singer noticed you, a song could follow. It might rub a raw edge too. When I was first brought to a club, my companion and I were assumed to be English, and a song began. "We all know the English.

They love their dogs more than their children.

How do we know?

Because when they go out they take their dogs and leave their children home. If they don't have a real dog do they go without?

No, they have to buy a toy one and hang it in the window of their car!"

Then he imitated the swinging dog - to the crowd's delight. Only later did I learn how dogs are loathed there.

I'd got off easy, wondering what he might have said about Americans!

That Wonderful Somebody

This was good entertainment. But Shata was also prized for public-spiritedness and for his courage, putting into edgy songs what the public most wanted to hear. With the country under Military Rule - a tense time. And one song had put his life at risk: so these days his two aims were keeping his fans happy and covering his tracks.

While the powerful courted his praise, and gave him gifts of cars and houses, they were also wary of him. His mercenary District Chief, an Emir's son, was outraged by Shata's song comparing him to the scoundrel in a folk-tale. Many told me how this Chief once turned a gun on Shata, who just replied, "Here am I, kill me then!" Fortunately, the Chief's companions restrained him. But now this 'greedy prince', who had got the song banned from radio and was now suing Shata for libel, had only whetted the public's appetite. The furore over the song kept the singer constantly in demand and on the move, only safe in the district of an Emir of Daura, a powerful supporter. The hottest items in the market then were private tapes made at his performances - which Shata encouraged.

When I met him I asked about the libel suit. "He can ban Version 2 anytime he wants - I already have version 3 ready. They can ban it all they want - I will always have more to say!" chuckled Shata.

While this song refused to be killed, I knew of another that refused to be born. For years Shata had refused to sing for the Military Governor of the province of Sokoto - a key province in Nigeria's political life. By chance I had been in Sokoto when its Governor managed to catch the singer - the Governor convinced he could now make Shata sing in praise of him.

As we talked Shata told me: "In the past - before Military Rule - I would sing for leaders but I don't sing for present leaders. And I don't sing for Military Governors…"

"So I heard," I interrupted, "I was in Sokoto recently…"

Shata looked pleased. "You were there?" I nodded. "You came to the club?"

"No, but after you were captured the whole town was full of rumours - I heard what you'd done from a broadcaster, Aminu, the next day."

Beaming and passing round some bottles of beer, Shata settled back in his chair saying, "Aminu's a good man. Tell me what you heard."

That Wonderful Somebody

"Aminu said you'd slipped into Sokoto hoping to escape the Governor's notice. You and your group were checking into a humble hotel when suddenly - sirens blaring - a long military convoy raced through the streets. In terror people scattered, fearing a coup. But the convoy drove directly to this small hotel, arrested you, careened back - sirens blaring again - through the streets and hauled you before the Military Governor. Word spread like wildfire... 'the Governor has caught Shata at last!'"

Shata nodded. "After years of trying!"

"And he demanded you make a song praising him."

Shata smiled. "As he had always wanted!"

"But as people tell it, you argued you would need a day to compose a song worthy of such an outstanding Governor. You claimed you wanted the song to 'do him justice'. You argued that - so as to 'give your best for such an event' - you and your group should be housed in greater comfort, and be paid in advance. Anticipating your song, the Governor agreed, handing over a good fee, and booking you into Sokoto's best hotel."

Shata was clearly enjoying this, nodding at the others in our group. So I continued...

"The public, shocked to see you carried off by a military convoy, now watched, wide-eyed, the same convoy depositing you - free of shackles - at the entrance of the Hamdullillah Hotel. They asked each other, 'could Shata have sold out? If the Governor is treating him so well, has Shata agreed to back Military Rule?'"

I went on. "I know that, no matter where you show up, your grapevine has spread the word. So that night Sokoto's best club was packed - and not just with your supporters - others came to hear how you would sing under this threat. Of course the Governor's men were there too."

"Naturally," agreed Shata.

"When you perform at a club I'm told you usually sing for up to 7 hours."

Shata nodded.

"But that night, after just two or three hours, claiming you needed a cigarette break - you did a runner! Your fans helped you evade the guards

Barbara Peterson

- and you slipped away into the night. And didn't surface again until you'd reached a very distant state, well out of the Military Governor's reach."

Shata beamed.

"Is that how it was?" I asked.

"Near enough," said Shata, laughing. "But there's something else... Did you hear that the governor had phoned Nigeria's other Military Governors? He was boasting he had finally got me - Shata, the greatest - to agree to praise him."

"I didn't hear that."

Shata went on. "My spies say I made him a laughing-stock. Yes, Sokoto's Governor - he's still very angry. That Governor has a great capacity for revenge and Military Rule shows no sign of ending. So I admit that my Sokoto fans will be deprived of my talent for a time.

"But never mind. Last week I was welcomed in neighbouring Niger. My fans filled a football stadium there. The song I wouldn't sing in Sokoto - that's history now. Niger wanted the songs I'm banned for! I even gave them Version 3."

Knowing that fans and broadcasters feared the current stress was killing him, I couldn't help what I said next. "Just now, in your own country you're always on the run..." Shata interrupted. "For telling the truth. That Chief's family want him to stop the lawsuits. I'm glad for them to continue."

I started again, "But in the next country..."

"They gave me five cars," said Shata.

....

Update: *Shata died in 1999, but interest and debate over his songs continues on the web, one fan writing: . "Oh! Shata is no more, but we still remember him for his courage to tell the truth to our leaders." But the web notes that under Sharia law, most of those wanting to keep the ancient tradition of praise-singing alive can only perform outside their homeland.*

Shirin Ramzanali Fazel

I am an Italian writer of Somali and Pakistani origins.

Author of Lontano da Mogadiscio (1994) and Nuvole sull'Equatore (2010) a novel which deals with the question of race discrimination, a crude legacy of the Italian colonial government. I have also published several short stories.

"Far from Mogadishu" in 2013 was reissued by Laurana Publishers in e-book bilingual format , translated and rewritten in English by myself where I expand on the painful issue of the Somali diaspora.

Currently engaged with the University of Warwick I am working on a project "Transnationalizing Modern Languages".

I have just completed the self-translation and the re-writing in English of "Nuvole sull'Equatore /Clouds on the Equator".

Foggy dreams under the sunshine

It is a salty warm night. The full moon is hanging in the clear sky like a huge Chinese lantern. There are no mosquitoes flying around this time. You can hear the croaking sound of frogs, and the chilling squeaks of long-tailed bush babies swinging from trees.

Sheila is immersed in the empty pool. She is floating. She looks like a lost duck. Gentle waves all around her. It is as if they are following the music playing in her head:

> I was waiting for so long
> For a miracle to come
> Everyone told me to be strong
> Hold on and don't shed a tear.......

Foggy dreams under the sunshine

Her lips are moving automatically, she knows all the lyrics of Celine Dion's songs. She wants to be Celine. For years she has been singing in front of mirrors and to her friends. Celine is an obsession.

Tonight her voice is carrying the pain she is feeling in her fragile, exhausted body. Around her the party is going on, in slow motion. Everybody looks so happy. Loud German accents clash with Bob Marley's "No, woman, no cry." Young men drinking Tusker beer from bottles shake their heavy dreadlocks. They are dancing with older women. Drops of sweat glide on their oily black skin. For her it is a grotesque movie. Familiar faces. The women are mostly Simba apartment residents. Europeans fleeing from the bitter cold winter to this tropical beach resort. Hans, the caretaker of the building, is here with his wife, Gloria. They turn to him if the washing machine needs to be repaired or if they want to book a safari. They trust him, it makes them feel secure to have someone around who speaks their mother tongue.

In Frankfurt or Cologne these women, dressed in their long woollen coats, would remain anonymous, taken for busy grandmothers. Under this mocking moon their aged bodies are covered only by light, colourful sarongs, leaving relaxed bellies exposed; hidden tattoos, heavy pink breasts and flabby thighs ravaged by varicose veins.

They look so childish with tiny yellow, green and red beads hanging from their long, woven, fake braids; lost in their love fantasies that only money can buy.

Sheila knows she does not belong here anymore. She wants to disappear. Her mind is travelling far away. She stayed for Raymund's birthday. He is sixty, only the wrinkles around his eyes betray his age. His body is lean, the result of many years of jogging at dawn on the white beach. Short grey hair. His face graced with a goatee beard. Sharp thin lips. He can speak for hours but never smiles. He is always so composed. That is maybe why she fell in love with him the first time she met him at the hotel where she was working as a receptionist. He was not like the other, vulgar, male tourists who would drool like hungry dogs over a female. His manners were so polite, he complimented her with grace. Their first dinner was a grilled lobster and a bottle of wine. She let him order and did not want to tell him "I have never had lobster. Our fishermen bring tafi to the village, a cheap fish full of bones that people can afford." Exhilarated from her drink she displayed all her dreams: "I will be a famous singer one day, like Celine Dion."

"Sheila you have every chance of becoming a pop artist."

Foggy dreams under the sunshine

She felt thrilled, a mzungu, a white man telling her she had talent. It was amazing.

"Sheila, come and work with me. I am opening a business."

From a temporary office in town Raymund ended up having his workroom at his new house at the beach. The mornings he spent at his computer, setting programmes and designing websites. Evenings they went to discos, restaurants or for a drink to other mzungus' parties.

He never attempted to pick up a woman, even when he drank a lot. Sheila would invite them home so Raymund could take some photos. It was part of his business, he told her. He wanted to help these young ladies to find a wealthy husband.

Sheila believed him; time was passing and the white prince never came to rescue these girls away from their misery.

Sheltered in her cocoon Sheila became lazy and enjoyed the beautiful life she had: a nice car, stylish pretty dresses, Italian shoes, a cook, a maid, a villa with a swimming pool and a peacock strolling behind leafy trees.

His daughter came for a visit. Linda, an interior designer, was almost her age. Sheila couldn't understand how this beautiful blonde girl could lie down at the pool the whole day, dying to have a tan. She hid from sunlight, feeding her body miraculous expensive whitening creams.

Raymund was boastful when he caught men's longing eyes brushing across his woman's figure. They envied him. Sheila was not like those girls picked up from cheap bars. Her manners betrayed her middle-class family. Her father, the only veterinary in the village, could not bear the idea of his daughter wanting to be a singer. He planned for her to be a teacher or a nurse. That is why Sheila left home one day, without a goodbye.

She had been with Raymund for almost five years. He promised her: "Sheila I will help you to find the right people, soon you will record your first CD. It will be a hit. Be patient, I want the best for you."

Things changed when she wanted to go to Nairobi for an audition. He discouraged her:

"Careful, my darling, those managers will promise you the world only to take you to bed. They know that girls will do anything to be famous. Sheila, you are not ready now, you have to practice more and more."

Shirin Ramzanali Fazel

Sheila was losing her confidence. She was no longer singing in front of a mirror, she had no friends. She would hum in the empty rooms the songs she loved. When she first got pregnant she was so uncertain. She wanted her man to reassure her, but Raymund's eyes were gloomy: "Sheila, we can't have a baby now. What about your career? I am still building my business, I am not ready yet."

The private clinic where she had the abortion was quiet and mostly for foreigners living abroad. Doctor Kumar had the same cold eyes as Raymund.

The second time she had a miscarriage, Raymund was in Nairobi for business. When he came back she told him: "I lost our baby."

She saw the light of relief in his face. Not a word he uttered. She tried to convince herself that what she was thinking was her imagination: "He loves me, he wants to have our child."

During the rainy season the sky got angry, rolling thunder poured hammering drops of rain. A huge rainbow would appear, the blue sea was calm and there was only the occasional tourist. Time was passing. Sheila felt a loneliness that was all-consuming. Raymund kept his routine as usual. She could predict his every gesture. There were no more surprises in her life. Even the cook had established the menu of the week. Mondays, tomato soup and crab salad for lunch!

Deliberately she "forgot" to take the pill. When she missed her period, she was happy. Sheila hid the morning sickness. His cologne made her nauseous but she tried not to show her disgust. After she was discovered Raymund did not wear his mask. His voice lost the fake calm tone:

"Sheila, I want to sell the house. My business is not going well, and after 9/11 tourists are not coming to this country. I have to leave; I will come and get you when I have settled in Madagascar. You can't have a baby now."

This time Doctor Kumar's eyes were as sharp as the knife she felt in her womb.

Everything around her was making her sick: the music, the laughter, the smell of barbecued chicken and fags. A small voice whirling in her thoughts:

"I hate myself for what I have done."

Tomorrow is a new day. Her suitcase is ready. She has arranged for a taxi to drop her at the airport. She is going to Nairobi. Raymund does not know. He will be jogging on the white soft beach.

David Rollason

I have been writing seriously for about six years after many years of inactivity.

Most of my early work tends to be about myself and certain issues that have run through my interesting if unconventional life but it is a life that has proved to inspire the wider art of my creativity.

After a marathon of self-publishing a memoir depicting specific aspects of my life, I now enjoy the freedom to explore different writing styles and subjects, taking inspiration from the wide and bountiful world that we live in.

Since joining Writers Without Borders, the eclectic mix of personalities, thoughts, styles and enthusiasms have provided a great inspiration to widen my creative base and offered the chance to learn and develop many elements of the craft including improving the performance of my work.

The New Friend

The new friend was sure to arrive on time despite the vagaries of train timetables.

Although no agenda had been agreed other than meals and a comfortable bed, a half-formed plan had always lurked in the shadows of his expectant, even hopeful mind.

The meal was prepared, a bottle of wine chilling nicely, the bed turned down, the time ticked on.

The morning brought relaxed birdsong and a comfortable feeling, getting milk for cereal, the wine jangled in the fridge door, the cling film covering the salad bowl glinted and speciality bread was used for toast.

For one.

Monumental

Stark stone slabs of cool mellow cream
hold secrets that, from far off, can't easily be seen
but hold them covetously they most certainly do,
and climbing the neat green bank you get just the hint of a clue.

From way off the smooth monolith stood boldly impressive
but as you get closer its monumental status is coldly oppressive
its scale designed to be forever imprinted on every eye
in the the names of lost souls, not all of whom needed to die.

Inside immense over-lifesize bronzes fashioned to represent
us, the living
stand tall as stiff reminders of fallen comrades in their
ultimate giving
the detailed power of the statuesque beauty crafted as hard-skinned clones
manage to give a tangible link for the lives now cold cut,
uniformly into the stones.

First impressions stored away, the wider, sadder sights are
soon overtaking
as every heart maybe outwardly bold, quietly, inwardly, each
one is quaking
as all around you from this magnificent bold bronzed
epicentre
stand the chilled columns of those lost from centuries of
calculated misadventure

Stark stone slabs of mellow mottled creams
display what's left of the thousands now, sadly, only held in
dreams
unless you knew one or loved one or perhaps felt that you should
have been one,
they're left chiseled and alone to be remembered, still, know that
they are gone.

The Cross

Rough-hewn, now old and battered wood lies blood soaked and splintered,
punctured with holes, stained rotting sinew, foul stinking and sintered.
Thrown to the ground after being dragged stuttering up to the hill...
now a scourged arm is stretched, full length, a soldier's grip holds it still.
The crowd simmers for the hammer that's lifted for only the first of the blows,
their cries ring out in cold, misplaced, blood lusted thirst, carrion crows...
watch square forged nails, mangled tips glint, once more sharpened
but when that first blow is struck, the mood changes, more real, hard, darkened.
No cry from the victim of this harsh, homicidal, capital attack,
but his hand clenches, eyes roll and an arch rises along his back.
The nail drives through fine skin, then into bone right down to the wood,
what worse fate can human lay on human, honesty, who ever could...
imagine worse, but, then the second arm is pinned and last, dirt-covered feet
crossed to receive pain while ranks sound a tattoo on their shields, a steady beat.
Then it stops, but still no victim's word as the cross is hoisted up on high,
the only sound now from a mother, but only then a small and muffled cry...
for her son who had not been given long in this savage, unremitting world,

David Rollason

she could only watch as the pain showed now, through his fingers as they curled.
As if it wasn't enough to contend with, during this vile humiliation
one warder, feeling guilty, takes a small sponge soaked in a libation,
obnoxious, crude, the guilt's compounded as he offers it up with a snigger,
spiced unkindly with mouldy sourness, in the form of rancid, acrid vinegar.
With the victim's weight overcoming what little strength he might have left
comes the first cry, not pain but pleading, it would leave him hanging, bereft,
'Why forsake me my father?' comes the cold, heart-wrenching exhortation,
'Forgiveness for all men, please', a last wish for our lives, his final act before total desertion.
Thunder cracks, his crowned head falls, the thorn-pricked bleeding now stopped,
lightning spears from the heavens and to the ground, the onlookers dropped.
Dressed in her blue, a mother pleads for the shattered body of her boy,
not even this travesty heaped upon her heart could a mother's love destroy.
The crowds wail loud, rent their clothes, shed cold tears while accusations fly,
from the ranks steps a lone soldier who claims, from this shameful act, he's now their ally.
With the body borne away, now lying empty, that simple blooded, wooden cross...
just like our wider world, can't possibly appreciate the consequence of this cruel loss?

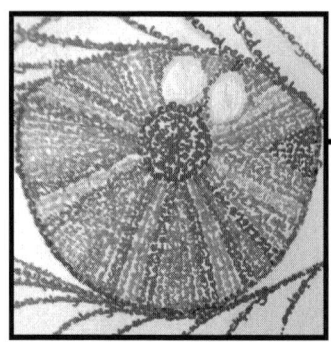

Sindy Stanley

My name is Sindy Stanley and I would describe myself as a crafts person.

When I grow up I'd like to be a painter and writer as well. I've written poetry but most are songs that float in on a tune that I tend to hear when I wake up, but I have to pretend to get back to sleep so that I can hear the words! Stories are harder because if I'm not careful they tend to write me.

In this contribution to the anthology, the name Pandara means 'wife' and Nonyemako means 'patience'.

Pandara's Box

"Where's the box?" Jen called, running up the stairs. She listened for the answer on the top landing. Dad came into the hall to say "Attic" in his usual way with a wink. Another flight later Jen stood in front of her childhood box and took a breath before kneeling in front of the only object she knew that held so many memories, mysteries and buckets of anger. Brushing the dust away from the top made her aware that her memory was contradicting what she found. The scribbles were not hers and looked like Mum's handwriting. Why didn't she understand what it said? Dad needed to explain a few more things than she thought. Jen reached the landing and realised the once treasured box had really changed; a darker shade of green, two different handles on either side and a lot lighter to carry. Ah, Mum's initials expertly calligraphed: P. J. B.

Dad carried in two mugs of tea and placed them on the table by the new-found box. Jen waited. They both sat opposite each other. Jen wasn't sure why, but she didn't want to miss anything Dad said or how he said it. After all, this is how it's going to be from now on she thought; just me and Dad. Her mother had gone and only left a strange letter. Maybe there were some answers in here they could both discover. Or maybe she really wasn't the person Jen thought she knew. A lot had happened to her since college, job, new flat, new friends. It made her feel sad and cross that there was so little she could do to repair the gaping hole where one parent should be. Death she could understand, but taking an unknown job in a different country with no forwarding address was a shock to say the least. Could she really trust those words? Was she unfaithful to Dad instead? With so little information to go on, who on earth had told her own mother to "get lost"?

Half way through his tea Dad opened the box and explained in a matter of fact way why Mum had taken over Jen's box. It didn't matter to her any more that it wasn't hers. She'd moved on. A bit like Mum she thought, biting back the anger she really felt. Peering over the lid she could see Mum's night classes clearly all over the interior. One by one Dad told a droll story to fit each object. This felt familiar; like being five years old again and prompting stories from Dad with objects she'd pick up from all over the house because he'd forgotten to pick up a new library book. She remembered the brass pixie which was connected to her Irish grandma. A miniature book with scrolled letters on each page, a battered Chinese cat

Pandara's Box

with one paw in the air that seemed familiar, but she couldn't recall the full memory.

Dad picked up the large iron key, crestfallen, lost in quiet recollection. When was the last time he saw **this**? 'How did she get her hands on it?' he thought. 'It's been here all this time? Oh no.' Dad let out a wounded sigh and slumped against his chair. Jen was talking to him and sounded anxious, distant. If only he could tell her how he felt, "be totally honest for once without judgement". His life was unravelling and he couldn't catch the thread to halt the bare-boned truth.

"Would you like a glass of whiskey Dad?" He nodded. How could he forget he had responsibilities? To himself, to Jen, but more importantly - to the one he really cared for. She wore silk stockings for his pleasure alone. He'd played with her feelings, her life. But where was she now? Could he really join her after all these years apart? The full glass of whiskey arrived and was welcome. He looked at Jen and saw pretty, smiling eyes staring back. It was time. With one smooth movement he placed the empty glass onto the table then held Jen's hand. A shiver climbed Jen's back as she began to realise Dad was trying to protect her from something. A bad decision? An argument? Lies? The truth? "Just tell me what happened Dad. I won't blame you or Mum. I just need to hear it from your point of view." Dad took a deep breath and leaned back.

"Do you remember Nonyameko?"

"No," she answered, thinking 'not another meaningless story.'

"Well, Nonyameko used to live with us before you were born", he began. "She was a refugee from South Africa. Her father ran a school there but he was killed in a guerilla attack. She was the youngest and most vulnerable, so her family paid her passage to England where she survived as best she could. She wasn't able to pay her rent because she was badly paid at the laundrette. That's where your mum met her as we didn't have a washing machine at the time. So we took her in. Your Mum was learning about her own family history at the time. She found a Grandfather from South Africa and Nonyameko helped her with the languages he would have spoken. His first language was Xhosa, which mum wrote on the box."

"What's that got to do with here and now?" said Jen mystified.

Sindy Stanley

"I'm getting to that. Nonyameko stayed with us for 2 or 3 years, then suddenly disappeared one day. We thought the authorities had got her. After all South Africa was a dangerous place then, she was very homesick and found it hard to settle here. Looking back it was a horrible time. But she left something behind. To this day I'm grateful for it. It changed my life. And your mother's."

"So what does it open? Where's the door it belongs to?" enquired Jen innocently.

"Er..........um," came the uncomfortable reply.

"Dad?" She raised the key to keep him talking.

"The key? Oh, the key was just a joke your mother and I played occasionally," he lied.

" 'The iron key has an iron will,' " she remembered. Click went the lock in Dad's memory.

" 'The railway line where there's still.......still...' " she struggled.

Dad's memory slipped back in time to see his own hand quietly turn the handle of the bedroom door.

" 'A canny way to hide your stealth....' " Jen remembered.

Closing the door behind him was just as quiet because it was where he wanted to be.

" 'And keep your heart instead of wealth.' I remember now, you used to show that to me at bedtime, or after a story, or something..." Jen froze. "There was a lady. A lady called 'Nonny'. She used to tell me stories and sing to me. I was very little. Mum and Nonny used to shout at each other. She had really pretty eyes, always smiling and ...." she broke off breathless, realising why.

"What did she leave behind Dad? You, or me?" Dad hung his head.

"Initially, she only left you. I was too self-centred to realise. There was a lot to consider. Your mother wasn't sure she wanted to keep you. You weren't hers and she wasn't sure about adoption. She wasn't sure about me either. Oh and yes, I am your father."

"So the joke was with Nonny, who is my....my....my Mother?" Jen stared at him aghast.

"Yes," he admitted. "But really, the joke was on me."

Sayyara Syed

I have lived and worked in Birmingham for nearly 45 years, having moved from Pakistan. I graduated in 1979 and started my career working for the Council. After having my daughters I went on to train as a teacher, working in higher education. I am now retired and enjoy writing, gardening, being a grandmother and spending time with loved ones.

Holding your Heart

These memories so clear in my mind,
Years and years apart, remain fresh in my heart.
I held you in my womb light
And later in my arms tight,
Not letting go of you, for a breath or a sigh,
Then you started walking
And holding my hand strongly.
There came a time you did not need to hold on,
You had the confidence to be alone.
And we were walking side by side,
Yet not being alone even when out of sight.
Now you've entered a new era,

Holding your Heart

A new beginning,
Opening a fresh chapter in your life.
You were in my mind,
I was in the shadow,
But holding your heart instead.
You and I determined and strong,
Stand next to each other, facing the realities of life.
We laughed, cried, struggled and flourished,
Holding each other's hearts,
Never being alone,
Even when out of each other's sight.
I am not forgetting the puzzle of your life,
I am still here
I am your shadow all of the time,
Holding your heart.
It has to change, and it will,
For you to flourish and strive.
But one thing is clear,
Although we may not hold each other's hand,
We do hold one another's heart.
No matter if we are far or near,
Love and respect will keep us together
In both our hearts and our minds.

Love

I have many questions in my mind about love,

I used to wonder if I would ever find love, I would ask,

Why do you create turmoil and upset in so many lives, leading lovers astray?

You ruin many hearts and homes, destroy them and turn them into deserts.

You break their hearts and lives.

They are forced to move from place to place punished for their love.

You make emperors shed tears and change kingdoms to dust and ashes.

One day by chance, I came across love, I was shocked and bewildered.

I fired all those burning questions boldly, the ones that have been eating away inside for the longest time.

Where have you been hiding?

Where do you live?

I have been searching for you everywhere.

Love held my hand and whispered gently in a sweet voice:

I live in every heart and grow there

I rule and direct the hearts of kings and queens.

Sometimes I turn beggars into wealthy men.

Yes it is me, yes it is me.

I live in the depth, in the depth of your heart.

I am a sea which has no boundaries, a limitless deep sea within one's heart.

Sayyara Syed

I am hidden and cannot be seen.

Only I spring out of a mother's heart like a holy light.

I grow in her womb to fulfil her dreams.

I raise generations, shape, mould and make them grow.

I hold myself back to protect the honour of my forefathers.

Sometimes I am a cord binding brothers and sisters by blood.

Sometimes I go through the test of time and have no fear of paying the price of my life.

As the legend goes lovers crossing rivers in a melting pot.

Sometimes I shine like the 'Taj Mahal'.

Mending broken hearts and dreams.

Sometimes I turn flames into blossom.

Sometimes I change a beggar to a prince.

I burn and become more precious and do not turn into ash.

Like gold turning into Kundan moulded with my fiery heat.

I do not burn others, I do not burn others.

I am love, love is my name.

I am not afraid of wandering from place to place

I have no fear of separation.

I belong to everything in this universe.

I sprang out of creation.

I live in people and they live in me.

I live in rich, poor and deserving hearts too.

I am nothing but love. I am nothing but love.

Martin Underwood

I am a founder member of Writers Without Borders.

Although not a Brummie I have lived here longer than anywhere else.

Within my submissions here, I don't often write 'narrative' poems but recently hearing of the incident I found myself writing 'Escape' – which has a sort of twist in the tail. Nor do I often write villanelles (they're tricky!) but I did think this one works.

Five Haiku

    Into the curved blade
The swordmaster has hammered
    The ghost of a forest
(Samurai sword in Birmingham Museum):

    Rain across the city
In the square the Iron Man
    Leans against the wind

    Behind the shelled house
In the overgrown garden
    Washing is still hanging.
(Croatia 1995)

    In hot sun the wasp
Drinks from the tap's hanging drop;
    I'll wait a moment.

    Sitting on my lap
The cat watches my fingers -
Then decides to helbbbbbbbbbbbbbbbbbbbbbb

If music....

It is born with them, the rudiments of song....
U.A. Fanthorpe

Some, before they learn to speak, can sing.
It is born with them, the rudiments of song
It irradiates the motion of their thinking.

It strengthens through the natural force of growing,
Expands like any flower, moving on....
Some, before they learn to speak, can sing.

And though speech follows, there is nothing
Clouds that innate overflow of song,
It irradiates the motion of their thinking.

Thought may spurn the natural urge to sing, -
Muffle it with logic - but not for long
Some, before they learn to speak, can sing.

As alien to the earth-bound as is flying
Music may be, yet reasserts itself ere long.
It irradiates the motion of their thinking.

The golden spiral with its music winging
Is, to generations not yet born, passed on;
It will irradiate the motion of their thinking.
Some, before they learn to speak, will sing.

Escape

Knocking at 2 a.m.
- a stressed whisper outside: 'They're coming'.
The urgent gathering of a few things
The group clustered in the foyer
The sounds of hasty vehicles in dark streets
The lines of light searching the sky
for glowing jetsam floating down
like dandelions and we are led,
He said he was from the Embassy
but he showed us no papers. We didn't ask.
Through the streets where gunfire
could be heard - big guns, distant,
small arms, closer, and the vehicle
stopped, checked, turned back, reversed,
sidestepped down to the harbour where a ship,
perhaps, might be, and might, perhaps,
get away unharmed in the dark.
No lights and yes, the iron ship there
and we on board hastily with no
recognitions or niceties of papers
our escort's presence enough guarantee
and then he on the quay, raised arm -
a salute? A farewell? What became of him?
Down then instantly into the hold banged shut
the engines going already and louder here
all of us thrown together in the metal dark
not knowing even if we were going
in the right direction, our only co-ordinates
the up and down indicating movement.

Martin Underwood

No facilities, food, little water, but just
holding on to a voice we recognised
or clinging to a more or less stranger
for what comfort there was in that.
Not knowing how long the slammed shut
night would be or had been -
and dozing not helping with the knowledge
and sense of how long time had been - until
at the end the engines slowed to a hesitating murmur
the movement smoothed to a slow slewing.
We have stopped somewhere.

One hatch opened. Cold air.
A voice. No questions. No answers.
A first glimpse of a paler black
and a few incoherent stars.
Which night is this? Where?
Have we escaped the war?

Based on the experiences of the English National Ballet company (Later the Royal Ballet) in 1940 who were on a goodwill tour to (neutral) Holland, when it was invaded on Sunday 19 th May at 02.00 by the Nazis without war having been declared. A British Embassy official managed to get them onto the last boat but one to leave the continent. The company included Ninette de Valois, Margot Fonteyn, Robert Helpmann and Frederick Ashton. All décor and costumes etc. had been abandoned after Saturday night's gala performance.

Farideh Valigholizadeh

I am Farideh Valigholizadeh

Energetic, creative, athletic and short

Strong, brooding, compassionate and considerate

Daughter of Iran, the land of torture and tears

A land consumed by oppression and fears

Farideh, the lover of a lost passionate time

Devotee of an embrace of sorrow that hasn't given pause to her life

Who is cold with herself in this disturbed time

Yet able to give love, friendship and warmth

For whom the meaning of the world is in her sob

Who stands in the dark to recall herself

Who meets herself in frozen hours

And dances with her shadow

To the last hit of pain and faints.

Helpless blossom (for my beautiful mother)

Windows frozen
With the breath
Of amnesia
The absence of memory
Is nodding gently

Like a frost
That lasts for a day
The city of her health
Buried in the dust of a doorway

She listens
To the echo of autumn
Her body condemned by age
As wind grows rage

I see her through
The crystal of my tears
Moving like a helpless blossom
Unable even to complain
The mirror shows no longer the same.

The moments I no longer touch

I touched the moment
Of richness
When I stopped time in your eyes
And reached to the skies

I lay on a bed
Of clouds
When the shouts of the day had died
And you stepped inside

I got lost
In the heart of your lips
When I buried myself in your fingertips
And the night glistened with frost

I grew greener
Became numb to ice and winter
When trees undressed in the cold
And dreams were put on hold

I had a flowing river inside
When I floated
On the black ocean of your body
In my devotion

I was saturated with your charm
Free from any harm
When you drank me
And drained off the colour of my soul

Let it rain

Let it rain
On my remains
Even if the city drowns
And the breeze dies down
To give the breath of life
To overcome any strife

Let it rain
On my remains
To plant a kiss on my cheek
In my journey you seek
To resuscitate
Once the oceans of thirst devastate

Let it rain
On my remains
Silence is beating down my brain
The oceans of hearts drain
since the worms of faith crown
The youth of this town

Let it rain
In my sleep with your heartbeat again
To take the bird's ease away
Like a frost that lasts for a day
Let it rain
The sky is pregnant with pain

Fiona Wallace

I started writing poems when I was a teenager and I would also draw back then. Sometimes people say my poems are like paintings. I lived in Greece for twenty-five years and used to go to a women's writing group there. We met twice a month in a beautiful, peaceful house and had to write on the spot.

I joined Writers Without Borders in 2008 when I came back from Greece. I suppose I write about the pull of two different cultures and two very different landscapes. Loneliness and longing come into it too.

Swallows

I left when the swallows came,
their soft undersides showing
as they perched on the nest edge,
no room inside for the long tail.

They'd been looking at it all week,
their old nest outside the front door,
confused by the paint around the rim
left by the workers last summer.

They're home again, back to the same spot
after a long journey over the desert,
here to make someone else's home,
my daughter's, more homely.

Swallows

May the birds be a good omen,
this spring and for many yet to come.
May they remind her only this matters:
the rhythm of the years,
the bringing up of young.

I head for the airport again
through olive groves and yellow flowers,
to fly north, to go home.

Bonfire Night

The hordes keep coming,
streaming down the path
towards the dark lake.
The fireworks are orgasms
that burst and slowly fade.
The brightly-coloured spheres
dazzle, twinkle and fall.

Still they keep coming,
down from the Lyndhurst
and up from Castle Vale.
They speak many languages.
Their children, in pushchairs,
hold magic sticks that glow
red, blue and green in the night.

They press on towards
the source of the light,
to where the music alternates
between pop and patriotic.
They flow on towards their goal,
an unstoppable river of dark shapes,
never pausing to look up.

I came back

I came back and the buddleia was out,
the garden full of butterflies.
England feels like home.
I'm at ease in its tattiness,
on the rather run-down bus
with the friendly driver.
I'm welcomed home by
the lady with a shopping trolley
and comfortable dress,
who gets on as a dog gets off
and tells me about all the pets she's had.

Is this where I've been living?
The house always looks smaller.
I'm back to my limited existence,
but the bedroom is reassuring.

I remember the English family
in the queue at Munich airport.
The mother is naturally beautiful,
with long, thick, fair hair
and very white legs.
Her two teenage daughters
have equally long, thick, red hair,
big, blue eyes and pale freckled skin.
They aren't burnt by the sun,
but they've been.
The red spots from mosquito bites
give them away.
Their father, originator of the red hair,
stands back, lets the women negotiate.
All three women could be models,
but lack the vanity.

Fiona Wallace

Alone in a hotel room after two weeks of life,
after Vassilakis running along the hall, shouting
'Nanna!'
There's nothing lonelier than a hotel at midnight
- the black TV screen,
the messages about room service and the minibar,
the kettle and two cups,
the perfectly made beds,
the pristine bathroom,
the buzz of the air conditioning.
How can I sleep here
after Melanie's sofa bed in the hot living room?
I'm doubly lonely,
lost among the anonymous corridors
and closed doors.
Not a soul.

Going Home

The man on the plane
looks down hungrily
at the Greek coastline,
at an island with white houses
and the sea with its white horses.
His thick grey hair surely
was once very dark.
His warm pullover is snagged
and there's dirt under his nails.
He's a Gastarbeiter going back for Christmas.
When we come out of the airport,
the soft wind brings us
the smell of herbs and the sea.

Elaine Yap

Known as Miss Kitty, I am a mature writer whose inspiration comes from life with its everyday occurrences.

I take from not only my own experiences but mould my poetry to depict dramas and other emotive feelings of people with whom I have contact.

Love is the driving force behind my creations. As an artist is inspired before he paints, I am inspired by my surroundings and anything that is uplifting to the human heart, mind and soul as well as issues that require a voiced opinion.

Naked I come to you, Oh Lord

Naked I come to You, my God, my all
Without the trappings of power and might
You who see deep down into my soul, the very heart of me
You who fashioned me, made every cell and every part of me
You know the inner me, right from the very start of time.
Take Thou these arms, these legs to work for Thee.
Take these eyes, let them see only the good in others.
Take these ears, let them be focussed on hearing good and pure words.
Let the words fall from these lips for Your glorification.
Renew my strength each day, to go about each human task.
Help me appreciate my fellow men and practice diversity to the end.

Play me

Play me a tune on that old guitar
Let it resound wide and far>>>
O'er land, sea and tide
Forever in my heart to abide.

Take me back to the times on that
        Old dusty trail >>>
To picture that train on track, on rail.

Play me that tune that will help to <<<
Bring back the sound of them coyotes on prowl.

Show me the moon on a dark, star-spangled nite
Hold me so close real tight >>> ^ <<<.

Let me rest my head on your shoulders bare
        While you play me, dear.
Let's go for a dip in the free-running waters
Watch buffaloes in their hunt on the range
        Acting real strange.

Capture the feel of the Wild West
Play me the way that only you know best.

All of nature will blend in sweet harmony
With this precious memory .... Dearest.

        Dearest >>> Just you play me!

A Butterfly

A delicate butterfly did
Flit upon a lion's nose

To her the lion did say ~ on sight
"Don't come too close, I might Bite!"

So dainty butterfly stayed ~ in flight
"I know about your power, your might!"

"Your company is all I seek, a delight that's all
I am a creature great ~ you are just small!

This terrain is my common ground:
Fear no ill while I am around!"

To this the butterfly did reply...

"My life is short, I wish none ill
But to beautify this world ~ I do instil

Much thought of love and tender care ~ not wrong
Through blessings and the sweetest song

Recalling days when I was young,
Memories so good they make us strong.

I'll fly away without much care.
Knowing for sure that you'll be here.

For life with love has so much power
Proof of this is known each hour."

The Brook

Babbling brook, trips over itself
~~~ in laughter and tears.
no care in the world, no fears!

Days are fun ones
as it dances along banks
of lands that stay strong.

Follow it through ~ a delightful you.
Make of its pleasure as it comes into view!

Fishes are tickled as she swishes along
making fun of each created song.

Sparkling diamonds as she reflects the sun
bringing enlightenment to you - to everyone!

Myriad of colours show nature's hue
Delighting the mind as it tantalizes you

Uplifting the feel of that babbling brook
Capture the memory of that picture you took!

Vivian Yates

I have chosen the first three of these poems for the way they trace the journey I have travelled in my life that has made me who I am both as a writer and a human being, the fourth because of my passionate belief in human rights.

I write mostly from personal experience and hope that my openness and candour will resonate with the reader or listener.

Above all I love to perform my poetry to an audience, if possible with musical accompaniment; 'Witness' and 'The Father I Never Met' were written particularly with music in mind.

Witness
In memory of Mahmoud Darwish
Voice of the Palestinian people

   Eloquent witness to a people
      uprooted from the land of your forefathers
         exiled for sixty long years
            robbed of your right to return
               dispersed across many lands
                  your homeland a distant but constant dream
     Voice of resistance
        Sculptor of identity
     Keeper of memories
        Messenger of humanity
     Your words
        that have travelled and touched the world
   will one day take root in Israeli soil

Who Am I?

My father's seed was Polish
but the father who raised me
was born and raised in Vienna
so am I East or West European
or simply a Kentish maid?

With such origins I was surely bound
to cast off the constraints
of my insular Kentish village,
turn my mind outward to a larger world.

It began when I fell in love with languages,
first French, then German, above all Russian,
with the sounds of the words,
the literature, the people
till I longed to be a Natasha or Tatyana
riding in a horse-drawn troika
with my beloved Sergei at my side.

It grew stronger at university
when I fell in love with an African
and with Africa, its music
the drumming and the dancing
and the warmth of its people.

Now my path was clear
I was neither Kentish nor European
but a citizen of the world
a member of the many-coloured human race
and here in this multicultural city
sat with fellow writers
from so many parts of the globe
I have found my natural home.

The Father I Never Met

I know you were a refugee
one of thousands who fled Nazi occupation
to seek sanctuary here.
Your name was Stefan
and your Polish blood flows in my veins,
I have at times been taken for a Slav.

I know, I have your letters to her,
you adored my mother, wished to marry her
and when she chose another
whose future was secure
you chose never to see her again,
never to see me your child,
your only child.

I know you married an Englishwoman,
made England your home
and lived into your eighties as my mother did.
Sometimes I wonder how it might have been
had your future looked so certain then.

First Love

We all remember our first love.
Mine, I was twenty-one
his name was Smaïn.
We met as students in East Germany
and the attraction was immediate,
pulling us like magnets
laughing, dancing,
how light and playful we were.

First Love
―――――

Then came the night he shared his stories
of his people and their struggle,
his struggle, for their freedom
and entrusted them to me
so I should write them
for the world to read and know.

That night we became soul deep.
A mere ten days after meeting
we pledged to marry, stay together always.
It felt so right, so natural
yet did we know what we were pledging,
I from a sheltered English village,
he a committed liberation fighter,
could our love transcend such difference?

We never found the answer.
Within weeks the call had come to war.
I wrote letter upon letter
but from him there came a silence
I could only take for deathly
so I grieved and let him go.

As we grow older and look back upon our lives
we see the path we've walked more clearly.
As I look back I see how Smaïn changed me,
opened my heart and mind to a larger world.
Sadly I never wrote his stories
but they inspired me
to seek to make the world a better place
and our love, a love which comes but rarely,
remains a precious memory
I shall carry with me to the end.